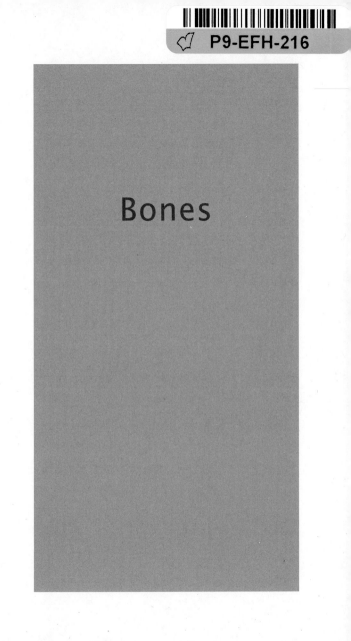

# Bones

# Bones

## John Wilson

*Orca currents*

ORCA BOOK PUBLISHERS

**Library and Archives Canada Cataloguing in Publication**

Wilson, John (John Alexander), 1951-, author
Bones / John Wilson.
(Orca currents)

Issued in print and electronic formats.
ISBN 978-1-4598-0710-5 (bound).--ISBN 978-1-4598-0698-6 (pbk.).--
ISBN 978-1-4598-0699-3 (pdf).--ISBN 978-1-4598-0700-6 (epub)

I. Title. II. Series: Orca currents
PS8595.I5834B66 2014      jC813'.54      C2013-906738-8
C2013-906739-6

First published in the United States, 2014
**Library of Congress Control Number:** 2013954152

**Summary:** Sam and Annabel learn about paleontology while solving a mystery.

*Orca Book Publishers is dedicated to preserving the environment and has
printed this book on Forest Stewardship Council® certified paper.*

Orca Book Publishers gratefully acknowledges the support for its
publishing programs provided by the following agencies: the Government
of Canada through the Canada Book Fund and the Canada Council for the Arts,
and the Province of British Columbia through the BC Arts Council
and the Book Publishing Tax Credit.

Cover photography by iStockphoto.com

ORCA BOOK PUBLISHERS
PO Box 5626, Stn. B
Victoria, BC Canada
V8R 6S4

ORCA BOOK PUBLISHERS
PO Box 468
Custer, WA USA
98240-0468

www.orcabook.com
Printed and bound in Canada.

17 16 15 14 • 4 3 2 1

*For Sir Arthur Conan Doyle,*
*whose* Lost World *first sparked*
*my interest in dinosaurs.*

## Chapter One

My mom meets us at the airport, wearing a poncho, a long paisley skirt and cowboy boots. Her hair is in two braids that swing wildly as she envelopes us in an enthusiastic hug. "Hi, Mom," I say as soon as I get a chance. "This is Annabel."

"Wonderful to meet you," Mom says to Annabel, then looks back at me.

"But you mustn't call me Mom. That defines me by the role of mother—a role I love, but I'm more than that. You must call me Acacia. It's a healing herb. Very good for skin ailments," she says with a pointed look at the huge zit that has exploded on my chin. "It also cures allergies, insect bites and athletes' foot. And the beans are delightful with guacamole."

I stand rooted to the spot, half overwhelmed and half horribly embarrassed. Annabel isn't fazed. "Yeah," she says, "it's an astringent, like tannin. Did you know there are almost a thousand different *Acacia* species in Australia alone?"

"Really?" Mom says, linking arms with Annabel. "I must go there one day. Aboriginal Australians have a wonderful history of using medicinal herbs. They have many more routes to healing than we do." Any worries I had about Annabel getting on with my weird mother vanish.

Mom and Dad split up several months ago. Dad and I moved to Australia, where I met Annabel, and Mom moved to a communal farm outside Drumheller, Alberta. A couple inherited it and decided to dedicate it to alternative life-styles. About fifteen people live there in a house and a couple of trailers, growing their own food, raising goats and chickens and making their own clothes.

The idea for a trip to visit Mom during the July school break came from Dad. The money came from Annabel's Uncle Bill. He paid for our flights to say thanks for the part we played in getting the *Loch Ard* peacock back to his museum.

I was missing Mom, so I was fine with the idea. I was nervous that Annabel might not want to come, but the news that there was a dinosaur skeleton on Mom's farm clinched Annabel's deci-sion to join me. The skeleton had been discovered by a local farmer in a small valley—coulee, it's called in Alberta—and was being excavated by scientists from the Royal Tyrrell Museum. There was no way Annabel was going to miss out on seeing a dinosaur dig firsthand.

I follow Annabel and my mom as they traipse through the airport deep in conversation about botany and folk medicine, leaving me to drag along behind with the luggage. I'm happy that they're getting along. It's going to be a great holiday.

"So these are badlands," Annabel muses out loud. We lean on our bikes, looking out over narrow steep-sided, cactus-filled valleys that go nowhere. We are at Horsethief Canyon on the Red Deer River. Dusty misshapen hills and weird spires of rock called hoodoos create a sci-fi landscape. Even on the edge of the badlands, it's hot. I have trouble imagining what it must feel like down in those narrow valleys, sheltered from even the merest breath of wind. "*Hunger Games* country," she adds.

"I wonder if there's such a thing as *goodlands*?" Annabel continues. "If there is, it would be the opposite of this. There would be gently rolling hills covered in grass and fields of wheat. Maybe a few cows or sheep grazing happily in the distance between broad, shady trees."

"*Anne of Green Gables* country," I suggest, and Annabel laughs.

"I guess we should head down to the museum if we're going to meet that scientist," I say. Mom has arranged for us to meet Dr. Owen, the man who's working on the dinosaur on her farm. He has agreed to show us around the museum.

We push our bikes out of the parking lot and set off along the narrow paved road toward Drumheller. The wind whistles past as we wheel over the edge of the prairie and down into the wide, flat valley bottom. We slow as the road levels out, and we pass small farms and stands of willows. I can't imagine being happier than this, cycling along on a beautiful summer day beside Annabel. I'm trying to imagine this moment lasting forever when Annabel powers off, yells "Race you," over her shoulder and leaves me in her dust.

I'm panting and sweating when we eventually pull in among the cars, campers and tour buses in the parking lot of the Royal Tyrrell Museum. We chain our bikes and join the tourists going through the main doors. We explain that we have an appointment with Dr. Owen and are directed through the exhibition hall to where he will meet us, beside the huge *T. rex* skeleton that is one of the museum's treasures. As we wait, I stare up at the skeletal jaws lined with curved, razor-sharp teeth, some of which are as long as my hand. "He seems to be smiling," I comment.

"What makes you think it's a male?" Annabel asks.

"Um, he's really big?" I suggest.

"That doesn't mean anything," Annabel says. "There are many species where the female is considerably larger than the male. The male triplewart seadevil is a tiny stunted creature that can only live as a parasite attached to the much larger female."

I feel like a tiny stunted creature when Annabel comes out with stuff like this. She's not only smarter than I am, she's smarter than everyone I know put together. "What's a triplewart seadevil when it's at home?"

"It's an anglerfish. They can live in depths of six thousand feet in the ocean."

"And how many decimal places can it recite Pi to?" I ask, teasing Annabel about her obsession with learning the endless number.

"Oh, female triplewart seadevils are known to recite Pi to over one million three hundred thousand decimal places. Though the males can only manage five or six."

She says this so seriously that it takes me a minute to realize I'm the one being teased. "Okay, you win, but I doubt the male *T. rex* was a helpless parasite."

"Probably not," Annabel agrees, "and this one, male or female, is impressive."

"Actually, the female *T. rex* may well have been larger than the male." We turn to see a short, bearded man wearing a shirt and pants that seem to be mostly bulging pockets. "You must be Sam and Annabel," he says, stepping forward and holding out his hand. We shake. "I'm Dr. Robert Rawdon Mallory Filbert Owen, the museum's director of dinosaur research, collection and exhibition," he says with a grin. "Quite the handle, eh? I always give my full name. It seems such a shame to waste it, but everyone calls me Dr. Bob. I'm so glad your mom could set up this visit."

His welcome is interrupted by the opening chords of Deep Purple's "Smoke on the Water." Dr. Bob looks sheepish and digs into one of his many pockets. "First thing I ever learned to play on the guitar," he says, dragging out a cell phone and stepping away. "Excuse me."

"Dr. Bob plays classic rock?" Annabel says, her face breaking into a broad grin. "Cool!"

"Sorry about that," Dr. Bob says, stuffing his phone away in a pocket. "Technology is convenient, but it does make it hard to escape. Have you had a chance to visit the excavation site yet?"

"Not yet," I say. "We were going to go down yesterday, but the rain made it too slippery."

"Rain is unusual here in summer, and it does make moving around in the coulees difficult. We didn't have anyone on site yesterday anyway. The team is back working at the dig today. In fact, I was planning to go down to see how things are going after I've finished here with you. You're welcome to tag along."

"Sure, thanks," I say. I glance at Annabel, who nods. "What exactly is the skeleton that you found there?" she asks.

"Exactly?" Dr. Bob says. "That's a tough one to answer. At first we thought it was a large ornithomimid dinosaur, because the hands were grasping and very lightly built. We even hoped for some feather impressions, but that doesn't seem to be the case. It's more complex than we thought. It might even be a completely new species, though we mustn't count our chickens before they're hatched, eh?"

Dr. Bob and Annabel laugh out loud. I nod, not really getting the joke.

"Counting chickens?" Annabel says.

I shrug.

"The dinosaurs were birds.".

"Oh, right," I say.

"Not strictly speaking," Dr. Bob says, "but very closely related. Anyway, would you like a tour of our setup here?"

"Yes," Annabel and I say at the same time.

"Excellent. Follow me." Dr. Bob leads us over to a door marked *Staff Only* and ushers us through. I glance back and say a silent goodbye to the smiling *T. rex*.

## Chapter Two

The back rooms of the Tyrrell are a
different world from the areas the
public sees. There are no perfectly
mounted skeletons posed in front
of paintings of ancient landscapes,
or computer terminals where you can
build your own dinosaur. There are
offices, rooms cluttered with camping
equipment, drills and hammers,

and a large warehouse filled with steel shelving crammed with wooden boxes and white, oddly shaped packages.

"This is an exciting time in dinosaur study," Dr. Bob explains, waving his arms around with enthusiasm. "Amazing discoveries are made every day all around the world—China, Argentina, Africa and even here in Alberta. We're digging fossil bones out of the rock faster than we can study them. We need all this shelving to store everything until we can get around to examining it. Sometimes, that's years."

"But they don't look like bones," I say, hoping I don't sound too stupid. "They're mostly large white lumps."

"Great observation!" Dr. Bob exclaims. He slaps a pillow-shaped lump covered in black writing. "The bones are often fragile, and we find them in awkward places—hillsides, cliffs, quarries. And with the short summer work season, the priority is getting specimens dug out and protected. We dig out the bone and the surrounding rock and wrap it in burlap sacking and plaster of Paris. It's like the cast a doctor would put on if you broke your leg. A doctor would treat you the same way we treat dinosaur bones. We're dinosaur doctors." Dr. Bob laughs at his own joke.

I force a smile and ask, "So what's in this one?"

He leans forward and peers at the writing. "Ah, this is a thigh bone from one of the horned dinosaurs, maybe even *Triceratops*." He chuckles. "*Dr. Bob rocks, like Triceratops*," he reads. "Sometimes our students like to write on the cast. Not the best poetry, but if it doesn't interfere with the scientific information, I don't mind."

"Where's the rest of it?" Annabel asks.

"And there you have hit the nail on the head," Dr. Bob says. Our confusion must show on our faces, because he continues, "Most people think dinosaur skeletons come out of the ground complete. Not so, and I'm afraid it's our fault." He falls silent as if he regrets a horrible mistake he's made.

"How is it your fault?" I ask.

"You think all our skeletons out there"—he waves his arm in the direction of the display halls—"are complete?"

I'm not sure if he expects a reply. He goes on before I can decide. "They're not. They're composites, casts of bones from several different individuals. And where we don't have a bone, we make it up."

Dr. Bob smiles at the look of shock that passes over Annabel's face. "Oh, very scientifically," he says. "For example, if we have two pieces of a backbone, it's a good guess that the missing piece between them looked much the same. Our reconstructions are as accurate as we can make them, but some dinosaurs are only known from one bone."

"So there must be a lot of dinosaurs that we don't know anything about," Annabel says. "Dinosaurs where we haven't found that one bone."

"Exactly." Dr. Bob moves back into enthusiastic mode. "There must be thousands of them. That's the thrill that keeps us all going. What's inside the next piece of rock? Will it be something we haven't found before? Will it be something we haven't even imagined before?"

"Like the bones you're digging out on Mom's farm?" I ask.

"Ah, counting chickens again. Whatever we have there has some unusual characteristics, but we won't know for sure until we get the specimen back to the lab and clean the bones out of the rock matrix."

"But you said that can take years," I say.

"Yes, it can, but we do work faster if there's a sign that we're onto something unusual. Can't be in a rush in this job. After all, the bones aren't in a rush. They've been waiting for us for sixty-five or seventy million years. We do try to get the bones out of the ground and onto these shelves here as fast as possible. We don't want to lose them."

"Lose them? They're not going to walk away," I say in a weak attempt at a joke. No one laughs.

"Losing them is a very real problem," Dr. Bob says. "There's a lot of money in dinosaur bones."

"Sue!" Annabel exclaims.

"Exactly," Dr. Bob agrees happily.

I'm losing touch with the conversation. "Who's Sue?"

Annabel says, "Only the largest, most complete *T. rex* skeleton ever found."

"Discovered by a private company in the sixty-five-million-year-old Hell Creek Formation of South Dakota in 1990," Dr. Bob adds.

"There was a huge controversy about who owned Sue. The farmer whose land she was found on, the company who discovered her or the government," Annabel says. She and Dr. Bob are competing to fire information at me.

"A court case gave Sue to the farmer," Dr. Bob continues breathlessly, "and he put her up for auction in 1997, where she sold for—"

"Seven point six million dollars to the Field Museum of Natural History in Chicago," Annabel interrupts.

"We were lucky with Sue," Dr. Bob acknowledges. "There was so much publicity that the museum could raise the money to buy her. That meant she could be studied. That doesn't usually happen. Museums don't have limitless money, and if it's not *T. rex*, it's not news. Countless wonderful fossils"—a look of sadness flits across his face—"have disappeared into private collections where they can't be studied. Also, if the bones are not properly removed, we lose huge amounts of information about the world the animal lived in."

"Didn't they discover that Sue had a healed broken shoulder and ribs?" Annabel asks.

"They did," says Dr. Bob. "She also had arthritis, a parasite that left holes in her bones and a bone infection."

"Wow," I say, as much in awe of Dr. Bob and Annabel's double act as at the information. "A dinosaur skeleton sold for seven point six million dollars?"

"Yeah," Annabel says. "Incredible, eh?"

"So you see, there's a lot of money to be made stealing bones," Dr. Bob says, "and it's quite easy. Most fossil sites are in out-of-the-way places. A few hundred bucks can buy a lot of information from an underpaid, overworked museum employee."

I nod, remembering the billionaire Humphrey Battleford, who traveled the world to buy and steal works of art for his collection. I wonder if he's into valuable fossils. Annabel is thinking the same thing. "I bet Battleford has a few choice specimens hidden away in one of his mansions," she says.

"Battleford!" Dr. Bob becomes excited again. "What do you know about Humphrey Battleford?"

"We ran into him in Australia," I say. "Why?"

"He's a legend in the fossil black market. He has deep pockets and will dig a long way into them for a fossil that catches his fancy. He has a better collection of fossils than most museums, but no one ever sees it. Legend has it that he has an almost perfectly preserved *Velociraptor*, complete with internal organs and feather impressions in the rock around it." Dr. Bob's gaze drifts wistfully. "Supposedly," he adds, returning to us, "he also has the only skull of an otherwise unknown early human species."

"From what you say," I point out, "it's a lot of work to get a dinosaur out of the rock. No one could do that without being noticed."

"That's right," Dr. Bob agrees. "But there's nothing to stop a major dig being undertaken as long as the landowner agrees. Your mom and the others on the farm gave us permission to dig in the coulee."

"Someone like Battleford wouldn't be interested in the skeleton on Mom's farm, would he?" I ask.

"I hope not," Dr. Bob says. "People like Battleford seem to have networks of spies in areas where valuable fossils are found. If word got out that we have something unusual, who knows? But don't worry. If he's looking for dinosaur specimens, he's probably in China. That's where the most exciting finds are being made—and also, unfortunately, where it's easiest to steal fossils."

Annabel jumps back and crashes into me as a man pushing a low trolley suddenly appears around a shelf of boxes. "Watch where you're going," he says.

"Careful," Dr. Bob says. "Where are you off to in such a hurry?"

The man is short and dressed in dark blue overalls. He has a square face and black eyebrows that meet in the middle above his nose. His head is shaved, but he has a goatee and moustache that match his eyebrows. Above the pocket of his overalls are the words *Paterson*

*Scientific Courier Service—Nothing Too Big or Too Small.*

"Sorry," the man says sullenly. "Got to take these out to the truck. Shipping them down to the Museum of the Rockies in Montana. All the paperwork's done." He waves at a clipboard of forms on top of the specimens.

"Okay," Dr. Bob says. "But be more careful. Those trolleys are heavy."

The man grunts and moves away.

"The best beetle eyebrows I've seen in a long time," Annabel comments. "He even has the sullen look to go with them."

Dr. Bob chuckles. "Beetlebrow— good name for him. He may not be the happiest courier in town, but he's the cheapest."

"Why do you send fossils to a museum in Montana?" I ask.

"We're short of space and staff, so sometimes we send specimens out to private companies for preparation and to other museums for research. Now let's go and look at the preparation labs."

As Dr. Bob shows us the rest of the museum's back rooms, I think of Battleford and his dog, Percy, and hope that they are as far away as China.

## Chapter Three

"I feel like a chicken on a barbecue," Annabel says, wiping the sweat off her brow with her sleeve. It's incredibly hot. We are in the dry creekbed of the coulee that cuts across the end of Mom's farm. Below us, where the dirt road ends, there are two Tyrrell Museum trucks, the one the field crew came in and, behind it, the one Dr. Bob brought us in. Above us, on the side of the coulee, a large square tarp shades a flat area where three grubby students in shorts, T-shirts and bandannas or wide-brimmed hats are huddled on hands and knees.

"Yeah," I agree. "Badlands trap the heat. I wouldn't want to come here without water." I haul my bottle out of my daypack, take a swig and pass it to Annabel.

"This is nothing," Dr. Bob adds cheerfully. "You can't get lost in a narrow coulee like this. In the big areas of badlands—over at Dinosaur Provincial Park or down in Montana, for instance—you can get turned around and spend a long time stumbling around. Then if it rains, you can't get out. The popcorn is like ice."

"Popcorn?" I ask.

"That's what we call the clay-rich rock here." Dr. Bob steps over to the steep valley side and scoops up a handful of irregular pieces of gray rock. They do look like popcorn. "When it dries out, it shrinks and forms this." He tosses the handful up in the air. "Popcorn. Of course, the opposite happens when it rains. The clay expands and becomes so slippery, you need climbing gear for a simple slope."

Dr. Bob points to the tarp. "Shall we go up and take a look?"

We scramble up the slope, and the students move back. The flat area is partly a natural change in slope and partly the result of some serious digging around three bumps. Two of the bumps are basketball-sized and are completely covered in white plaster. The third is about the length of a longboard and is half covered in plaster.

"Things are going well," Dr. Bob comments.

"Yeah, man," says one of the students, a tall skinny guy wearing a black bandanna with a skull and cross-bones on it. "We'll finish plastering the top this afternoon. We've almost dug out underneath. We should be able to turn them tomorrow, and then they'll be ready to truck to the museum on Sunday."

"We dig to find the extent of the fossil," Dr. Bob explains. "Then we plaster the top for protection, dig underneath, flip it over and plaster the bottom. Then we can transport it back to the museum and put it on the shelves you saw earlier."

The pirate guy takes a phone from his back pocket, steps away and takes a photo of the site. He catches me looking at him. "It's for the blog," he says. "I post a photo every day. This is important work, and people need to know about it."

"He's right," Dr. Bob agrees. "These days, we have to keep up with the technology, and the more young people who know what we do, the better. It's not all *Jurassic Park*, but if we give these bones a story, it helps people relate to what we're doing."

"What's the story here?" I ask, waving at the hillside.

"Seventy million years ago this was a coastal, swampy place, cut by rivers running into the sea over there." Dr. Bob points east. "Our friend here"—he kneels down beside the largest lump—"was washed down one of those rivers. His or her body got stuck on a sandbank and provided a meal for some small animals. That scattered the bones around a bit, which is why we have him in three lumps. I reckon we have about fifty percent of the skeleton. We're missing the hips, back legs and tail, but we have the backbone, ribs, front legs and, most important, some of the skull."

"What was it like?" Annabel asks.

"Hard to say. Probably something like a small ostrich, except with a long tail. This is one of the hands." Dr. Bob leans over the partly plastered lump and points at three long bones radiating out from a jumbled collection of smaller ones. "Very delicate. Probably good for picking fruit."

"But it's the skull that's really cool," says the pirate guy.

"Ah, yes," Dr. Bob says with a smile. "Captain Jack Sparrow here thinks we have a smart dinosaur."

"The skull," the student says, pointing at one of the basketball-sized lumps, "has eyes on the front, like we have, and a high forehead, which suggests a large brain."

"Apparently," Dr. Bob agrees, "but we can only see a part of it. We won't know what we're dealing with until we remove the skull from the rock. But you're right, this *was* a smart dinosaur."

"What!" I exclaim, thinking of a book I read about intelligent dinosaurs that talked to each other, built towns and tamed other animals.

"Smart for a dinosaur," Dr. Bob adds quickly. "Lots of them had eyes like ours on the front of their heads. It's a useful adaptation if you want to catch fast-moving prey or pick fruit off a bush. But a high forehead doesn't always mean intelligence."

"*Pachycephalosaurus*," Annabel says. "It has a domed head and looks smart, but the dome is just a bony lump. People used to think they head-butted, but the neck's not right. They probably used their heads to butt the flanks of their opponents, like giraffes do."

I stare at Annabel. How is there room inside *her* head for all that information? And what normal person knows that stuff about giraffes and that weird-named dinosaur? Of course, Annabel's *not* normal, which is one of the things I like about her—normal is boring.

"Your girlfriend is smart," Dr. Bob says with a smile. I blush violently, but I'm happy. Annabel *is* my girlfriend, and that makes me very lucky.

"I just remember stuff," Annabel says.

"Like Pi to some ridiculous number of decimal places," I say.

"Over four thousand now," Annabel says proudly.

"*Now I fall, a tired suburbian in liquid under the trees, drifting alongside forests simmering red in the twilight over Europe.*"

We all turn to stare at the pirate who has said this gibberish. He looks at Annabel.

"Pilish," she says.

"No need to be rude," Dr. Bob says.

"No," Annabel says, her excitement rising. "He's speaking Pilish."

The pirate nods, a self-satisfied grin on his face.

"What's Pilish?" I ask, feeling left out.

"It's the language of Pi," Annabel explains. "Count the number of letters in each word—*Now I fall, a tired suburbian in liquid under the trees.*"

I concentrate. "Three, one, four, one, five…it's Pi!" I exclaim.

I'm happy that I worked it out, but Annabel is talking to the pirate. "That's from *Not A Wake.*"

"Yeah," the pirate agrees. "The first book ever written in Pilish. The number of letters in each word in the book corresponds with the digits in Pi. It goes up to ten thousand decimal places."

"That's so cool," Annabel says. "I've always meant to read it but never got around to it. Have you read it?"

"Every word," the pirate says. "It's awesome."

Dr. Bob looks at me and shrugs. He feels as left out as I do. I am developing a dislike of the pirate who knows as much about Annabel's favorite topic as she does. How can I compete with that?

"But Dr. Bob, why couldn't this dinosaur be really smart?" pirate guy asks. "I mean, they evolved for over a hundred and fifty million years. And they would have kept changing if they hadn't all been killed sixty-five million years ago. Someone suggested that they might have evolved into something like us, walking upright, using tools— perhaps they even spoke to each other. Some animals today—chimpanzees, whales—have complex language. Maybe dinosaurs developed that before they died out, and we haven't found the right bones. Until now."

"That's stupid," I blurt out.

"Not necessarily," Dr. Bob says. "It's extremely unlikely that's what we have here, but in science we must keep an open mind. If we dismiss an idea as stupid, then we won't recognize evidence if we see it."

Now I feel stupid, and everyone is looking at me. "Let's go back to the farm," I say to Annabel, keen to get out of here and take her away from pirate guy.

Annabel looks surprised. "I thought we were going to hang out here longer. Maybe even help out. I'd like to stay."

"You can if you want," I say, more harshly than I intend. "I'm going back to the farm."

I climb out of the coulee onto the flat prairie and stop to catch my breath, hoping Annabel is following. She's not. I glance down, and my heart sinks as I see her crouched beside the pirate, looking at the fossil. Dr. Bob looks up at me and waves. I wave back half-heartedly and trudge across the fields toward the distant farmhouse. I feel horribly lonely, the only person in this vast flat land. Why did we have to come here?

## Chapter Four

My trouble is that I can't let things go. If something bothers me, I worry at it like a dog with a bone. I convince myself that the worst possible outcome will happen. I'll sleep in and miss the exam, or say the most embarrassing thing possible in front of the whole class. Right now, I'm seeing Annabel and the pirate guy strolling along the street, holding hands and laughing at an obscure Pi joke that I can't understand. They look perfect together. They are even the same height.

I kick a clod of dry earth in frustration. It was probably dumb to leave them together back at the dig, but if I'd stayed, I would have said something else stupid. I wish we were back in the diner in Australia, eating fries and talking about shipwrecks. That would be simple—and no pirate guy.

The rough sound of an engine makes me look up. A beat-up red pickup truck bounces toward me along the edge of the field. I watch as it slides to a halt in a cloud of dust. A guy in a plaid shirt and oil-stained baseball cap leans out the open window. "Howdy," he says. "Can I help you?"

"No, thanks," I say. "I'm just heading home." I nod toward the farmhouse.

"You one of them Australian kids staying with the hippies?" The hand-rolled cigarette hanging from the corner of his mouth bobbles as he talks.

"I'm Canadian," I say, "but yes, I do live in Australia."

"You been down at the bone place in the coulee?" he asks.

I nod and begin to walk away. I don't want to get into a conversation with this guy. Not only am I too miserable for small talk, but there's something about him I don't like. I think it's his eyes—they're small, set close together and shifty.

The dog that leaps up from the bed of the truck, barking, almost gives me a heart attack—for two reasons. One, I wasn't expecting it, and two, it looks like Humphrey Battleford's dog, Percy, from Australia.

"Careful. Ajax ain't fond of strangers." The guy in the truck smiles at my discomfort.

Once my heart slows down, I see that Ajax is actually not like Percy.

He's the same breed, a black Lab, but he's older, with a touch of gray around his muzzle. And his temperament is nothing like the friendly Percy's.

"Must be pretty near ready to lift that fella out," the guy says.

I turn back. "What do you mean?"

"The fossil fella down in the coulee." The truck driver removes the cigarette from his mouth and spits in the dust. "They been working on it long enough. I been following the blog that kid keeps. They ready to move it soon?"

"I guess so," I say. For some reason, I am reluctant to give him details.

"What d'you reckon it is?"

"A dinosaur," I say.

"Maybe so," the guy says. "Word in town is that them bone guys have found a smart dinosaur, maybe even an alien or some such. They're keeping quiet about it, but when word gets out, it's gonna change everything. Something like that'd be worth a buck or two." He rubs his thumb and fingers together in the sign for money.

I stare at the man. "It's an alien," I say. "His spaceship's parked down by the mall in town."

For a moment, the guy stares at me, his jaw hanging open. Then he laughs. "That's funny." He lets the clutch out and the truck jumps forward. I close my eyes and wrap my arm over my nose and mouth as the dust swirls around me. When it clears, I continue my miserable walk. That's two people now who have told me that Dr. Bob's dinosaur is special—smart or an alien or both.

"Where's Annabel?" Of course that has to be the first thing my Mom asks when I walk through the kitchen door.

"She stayed down at the dig," I say as casually as I can.

Mom looks up from the counter where she's rolling out dough. "Everything okay between you two?" She's always had this incredible radar about relationships. The only couple it didn't work with was her and Dad.

"Yeah. Yeah. Everything's fine," I say, reaching for a warm scone on the tray on the table.

"Just one," Mom says. "They're a new recipe. Whole wheat, blackberry and ricotta. I don't want you spoiling your appetite for supper."

"What's for supper?" I mumble through a mouthful of scone.

"Mac and cheese."

"Mac and cheese?" This doesn't sound like the sort of thing that's cooked at the commune.

"Yeah," Mom says, "with basil, broccoli and Gruyère cheese."

"Oh," I say. That sounds more like it. In the days with Mom, I've learned more about weird food than I ever thought possible. I've also promised myself not to ask what something is, because it always leads to a long explanation of why it's healthy. Not that I'm against food that's good for you, but I am going to be craving a burger by the time I go home.

"The scones will go well with it, and there's nettle salad."

"Nettle salad?" I ask, forgetting my promise.

"Don't worry—they don't sting once they're cooked. They taste like spinach. Very rich in vitamins A and C and in iron, potassium and manganese."

"I can't wait," I say to interrupt the flow of information. "Who's the creepy guy in the red pickup? He was driving around the field as I was coming up from the dig."

Mom grimaces. "That's Darren. He leases the field from us."

"But there's nothing growing there," I say.

"Last spring, Darren was full of all these ideas for growing genetically modified crops and getting rich. We pointed out the clause in the lease that said he could only use organic farming methods on our land and GMOs didn't fit the bill. He complained, but there was nothing he could do. He never got around to doing anything with the land—spends too much time with his no-good friends in the hotel bar. Still, it won't do the soil any harm to sit fallow for a season."

"He seemed interested in the dinosaur bones," I say. "Thought they belonged to an alien."

"Darren's a couple of nickels short of a dollar, if you ask me." Mom brushes the flour off her hands, comes around the counter and envelopes me in a hug. "I'm so glad you came to visit," she says when she lets me go. "I've missed you.

I thought it would be years before I saw you again. Are you settling in okay?"

"I am. School's weird. They're strict, and we have to wear uniforms and stuff, but everybody is nice."

"Keeping your grades up?"

"I am," I say with a smile. "You know me—solid B student."

"You'll do fine," Mom says. "As soon as you find something that interests you." She walks back to the sink and begins washing the baking tools. "I'm so glad you brought Annabel with you. She's a lovely girl, and that makes you a lucky boy."

"I have to go," I say, standing up. The last thing I want is for Mom to ask too many questions. "I promised I'd email a couple of friends about the dig."

On the way to my room, I look out over the field. Darren's truck is parked at the far end, but there's no sign of Annabel.

# Chapter Five

Annabel returns to the farmhouse in the late afternoon and is chattering with excitement about the dig. "They've finished plastering the top of the big fossil. They should be able to turn all three pieces tomorrow and plaster the bottoms. The day after, they'll be ready to move them back to the museum. It means working on Sunday, but Dr. Bob doesn't want to leave them exposed longer than necessary."

I'm trying to hide my worry about her and the pirate guy and act cool.

"Does he think they might get stolen?" I ask.

"I think so. The pieces are not huge—three or four guys could move the biggest one—and it's downhill to the end of the track where you can park a truck."

"Can't he leave a guard on it?" I say.

"I doubt Dr. Bob's budget would cover hiring a security company."

"Maybe a summer student could camp there and keep an eye on it."

"That's an idea," Annabel says. "I'll mention it to Greg and see what he thinks."

"Who's Greg?" I ask, although I'm sure I know the answer. This is not the way I wanted the conversation to go.

"The guy with the pirate bandanna. Though everyone calls him Jack Sparrow.

When they do, he always replies, '*Captain* Jack Sparrow,' like Johnny Depp in *Pirates of the Caribbean*."

"I know. I've seen the movie," I say, bitterness creeping into my voice.

Annabel looks at me oddly and then goes on. "Anyway, he's interesting. His blog is cool—some great shots of the dig and the stages of the fossil being prepared. He says there's going to be a barbecue down by the Red Deer River tomorrow night. Want to go?"

"Did the creepy guy in the red truck show up at the dig?" I ask, desperate to change the subject. I need time to think.

"Darren? Yeah. You think he's creepy? He found the dinosaur in the first place. Apparently, he's quite the amateur fossil collector. He sells samples to some of the rock shops in town."

"Just as well he didn't try and sell this one," I say.

"Luckily, he recognized its importance and went to Dr. Bob."

Darren being smart enough to recognize a fossil's importance strikes me as unlikely, but I don't say that. "He thinks the fossil's an alien."

Annabel laughs. It's a sound I normally find captivating, but not in my present mood. "He mentioned that," she says. "Greg says it's because Darren comes from a town called St. Paul in northern Alberta. Apparently, they have a UFO landing site there."

I stare at Annabel. I don't know what to say. Here is the most rational person in the world, cheerfully talking about UFO landing sites.

"I don't believe in UFOS," she says when she sees my look. "But, like Dr. Bob says, you have to keep an open mind. Do you want to go and wander round town tomorrow? There's a huge *T. rex* by the river. You can climb up inside and look out its mouth."

"Sure." I shrug. "But we left the bikes down at the museum."

"Maybe your mom can give us a lift into town. Didn't she say she was going to the market tomorrow?"

"Yeah," I say without much enthusiasm.

"Are you okay?" Annabel finally notices that I'm not at my cheerful best.

"I'm fine," I say. I'm saved from explaining further by Mom calling us for our nettles and Gruyère cheese.

The evening turns out better than I expected. Greg isn't a major topic of conversation. Supper with the other members of Mom's commune is okay, although some of them are so relentlessly upbeat that I doubt I could stand living there for long.

Afterward, Annabel and I skip the yoga session in the living room and watch *Jurassic Park* on my laptop. We play spot the flaws in the movie. I think I'm doing well by noticing that the goat being fed to *T. rex* is making noises like a sheep. Annabel blows me out of the water by pointing out that the mosquito in amber is a male and only the females drink blood. The male wouldn't have any blood in him, so they couldn't extract dinosaur DNA. I go to bed feeling no smarter but happier.

# Chapter Six

"This is so cool." Annabel leans over the rail to peer down at Drumheller between the teeth of the world's largest *T. rex*. She's so enthusiastic that I can't bring myself to mention how tacky this giant dinosaur statue is. We may be inside the biggest dinosaur, but it's not the only one. Drumheller has a dinosaur on every street corner, ranging from cartoonish to fairly accurate. I'm a lot less miserable today. Wandering about town this morning has been fun and relaxed.

"It is kind of fun," I agree, looking down at the forest of tourists in the parking lot below, all pointing cameras up at us. Small children are happily crawling over the *T. rex*'s toes. Then I notice the beat-up red truck in the corner of the parking lot. When I see the black dog in the back, I'm sure it's Darren's truck.

"I wonder how it's going at the dig," Annabel says before I can point out the truck. "Greg says there's a lot of work to be done today to get the casts ready for transport. Maybe we could drop by later and see how things are progressing."

My heart sinks. The last thing I want to do today is spend the afternoon with Greg.

"Darren's in town," I say to change the subject. As I say this, Darren and Beetlebrow—the courier from the museum—emerge from a café and saunter over to lean on the truck. Darren lights a cigarette.

"So Beetlebrow and Darren are buddies," Annabel says.

"It's a small town," I comment.

"I wonder who that is." Annabel points at a black Hummer that is turning into the parking lot. It pulls up beside the red truck, and Darren and Beetlebrow walk over and lean in to talk to the driver. In the back of the pickup, Ajax goes berserk, and I can hear another dog barking from the Hummer.

"Darren has some rich friends," I say.

The conversation below us doesn't last long. The Hummer pulls away onto Highway 9, toward Calgary, Darren calms Ajax and stamps out his cigarette, and he and Beetlebrow head off in the opposite direction.

"What was all that about?" Annabel wonders.

"Who knows?" I say, happy that we've moved away from a conversation about Greg. "Let's go check out that fancy rock shop we saw on the way here."

We climb down *T. rex*'s right leg and head for the fossil store.

The woman behind the counter in Precious Fossils and Gems gives us a chilly look. It's obvious that we can't afford much in this place. I feel uncomfortable, but Annabel smiles at the woman, says, "Good morning" and begins looking at the treasures.

The first thing I see is a slab of pale rock containing a perfectly preserved, two-foot-long fish. I can have it for my bedroom wall for a mere $3,500.

I try not to gasp as I wander around the store. The place is incredible. There's a complete saber-toothed tiger skull ($70,000), a small bird ($23,000), a squid ($28,500) and a weird spiny thing called *Quadrops* ($5,750).

The woman watches me like I'm going to slip a six-foot-long slab of rock containing a perfect shark fossil ($675,000) under my jacket and run for the door. The only thing in the shop that I can afford is a small curled shell for only $65. I'm totally mesmerized. There's obviously a lot of money in fossils.

"It must be a good area around here for getting fossils for your shop," Annabel says sociably to the woman.

"Not really," the woman replies. "The fossils here are mostly single bones and fragments, curios for the tourists. We're not that kind of shop," she adds snootily.

"But," Annabel persists, "if someone brought in something—an unusual skull, for example—you could prepare it and sell it?"

"We don't have the facilities to prepare fossils. There are companies who do that, mostly down in the States. So in the unlikely event that we acquired a fossil such as you suggest, we would ship it to them for preparation before we displayed it."

"So if you don't get fossils from around here, where were all these collected?" Annabel asks.

"All over the world," the woman replies with a fake smile. She's still watching me out of the corner of her eye. "For example, most of the fish come from the Green River Formation in Wyoming, and the shark that your friend is interested in is from Germany."

"Aren't they protected?" Annabel asks.

to us, but she is holding her cell phone to her ear.

"Okay," I say when we're past. "I owe you a plate of fries, but what did all that mean?"

"I was just being silly when we left the shop. I used Battleford's name to make the birthday present story seem more real."

"It certainly worked," I say.

"Yes, but why? As soon as I mentioned Battleford, we went from being a pair of annoying kids to a lost opportunity for a big sale."

"She knows Battleford!" I say in sudden realization.

Annabel nods. "And I'll bet a burger to go with the fries that it was Battleford on the other end of that phone call."

"I can't afford any more bets with you," I say, "but her knowing Battleford doesn't mean anything sinister is going on. He's a filthy-rich collector, and he's

certainly mixed up in some shady dealings, but that doesn't mean everything
he does is illegal. He probably buys
from places like this all over the world."

"I didn't say anything illegal was
going on. Though it's criminal that
such incredible specimens aren't put in
museums or given to scientists to study.
I do think it's odd that Battleford's name
keeps cropping up everywhere."

"You brought his name up," I point
out. I'm enjoying listening to Annabel
work things out.

"True, but she knew it and so did
Dr. Bob. Greg knows about him as
well. He was telling me about all the
incredible fossils Battleford owns. He's
supposed to have a fossil that proves the
link between dinosaurs and birds."

My good mood evaporates when
Annabel mentions pirate man. I'd almost
forgotten about him. "Fascinating," I say.
"Let's go and get those French fries."

Annabel gives me an odd look but follows me down the street to Dino's Diner. I order a brontosaurus burger and fries from a bored kid wearing a cap with picture of *T. rex* on it.

A tuneless piece of piano music rings out. Annabel tells me it's Pi if you translate musical notes into numbers and play them. It's no "Smoke on the Water." She flips open her phone and says, "Hi." I hope it's not Greg on the other end. She listens, nods a few times and finishes with "Great. See you tonight. Looking forward to it."

Please don't let it be Greg, I think.

"That was Dr. Bob," Annabel says as she flips the phone closed. I sigh with relief. "He invited us to the barbecue. We are going, right?"

"I don't know," I say, thinking the evening will be a complete bust if Annabel spends the whole time with Greg.

"Unfortunately, Greg can't be there.'

"Oh," I say, trying not to smile.

"He's going to be watching the fossils tonight. It's a shame he'll miss the barbecue."

"Yeah, a shame," I say, but it's nowhere close to what I'm thinking. "The barbecue sounds like fun." Suddenly, it does, and I tuck into my brontosaurus burger.

# Chapter Seven

"I hope you brought swimsuits," Dr. Bob says. "It's a tradition to go for a midnight dip in the river."

"It'll certainly feel good," Annabel says, and she's right. It's ten at night, and it's still hot. We're on the riverbank close enough to Mom's farm that we could cycle down. The sun has disappeared below the horizon, but the twilight is still bright enough to see the smoking barbecue pits and the inviting cool water winding its way between sandbars.

"Those ribs were great," I say, remembering how the delicious meat fell off the bones.

"A secret recipe," Dr. Bob says with a smile. "Although I think anything would taste good beside the river on a night like this."

"The forecast mentioned thunderstorms," Annabel comments.

Dr. Bob scans the sky. "It's possible. There are some thunderheads off to the west. Might develop, might not."

"Will Greg be all right at the dig?" I cringe at Annabel's mention of the pirate guy. It seems I can't escape him.

"He'll be fine," Dr. Bob says. "His tent is set up on the prairie, so he won't get washed away if it rains. It was decent of him to volunteer to keep an eye on things. I don't think anything will happen, but it can't hurt."

"He volunteered?" I ask.

"Yes," Dr. Bob says. "After Annabel phoned me and suggested it might be a good idea, I mentioned it. Greg volunteered straight away."

"You phoned Dr. Bob?" I say, turning to Annabel. "You never told me."

"It wasn't a secret," Annabel says. "After we talked about the possibility of the bones being stolen, I phoned Dr. Bob with the idea. I guess I forgot to mention it. Anyway, how about we ride up while there's still some light and see how Greg's doing? He must be lonely while we're all enjoying ourselves down here."

"I thought Dr. Bob was going to play us some classic rock," I say, in a panic over Annabel's suggestion.

"That is indeed true," Dr. Bob says. "I brought the guitar, and I play a mean 'Stairway to Heaven.'"

I look at Annabel with what I hope is a pleading expression. It doesn't work. Annabel becomes all businesslike. "Okay," she says. "Look, I'll pack up some ribs, pedal up the coulee and see how he's doing. I'll be back in half an hour. Don't play 'Stairway' until then."

"Deal," Dr. Bob says.

Annabel leans over, gives me a quick peck on the cheek and is gone.

"Quite the girl you've got there," Dr. Bob says.

I mumble "Yeah" and head along the riverbank into the deepening shadows. I need to be alone. What's going on? I can't escape Greg. Annabel and I will have a wonderful couple of hours and then, wham, there's Greg again—either in person or sneaking into the conversation. Is he taking Annabel away from me? If so, what can I do about it?

A black thought begins to take shape in my mind. What if Annabel and Greg planned this? What if the suggestion to Dr. Bob that someone camp out at the dig was simply a way to allow Greg to volunteer? What if Annabel planned all along to go and see him tonight?

This is ridiculous. Now I'm building conspiracy theories out of nothing. Annabel suggested that we *both* go see Greg. My stupid uncertainty kept me here. Hadn't she given me a kiss on the cheek when she left?

Maybe it was a goodbye kiss.

It's no good. Once the seed of doubt is planted, it grows like a weed. Feeling utterly miserable, I sit down on a rock and begin chucking stones into the river. There is nothing I can do. I've always known it was only a matter of time until Annabel met someone more suited to her intelligence than I am. I just wish it had taken longer.

"Hey, man, you can't throw stones in the river once everyone goes for a dip."

I spin around to see Greg coming toward me.

"What are you doing here?"

"Nice welcome. I came down to snag a couple of beers and some ribs to take back up to the tent. I don't think our fossil's going to run off in the next hour."

"Where's Annabel?"

"What?"

"Where's Annabel?" I almost shout. "She went to visit you. Didn't you see her on your way here?"

"She came to see me? Sweet, but I came over the prairie." Greg waves his arm upstream. "Didn't want to run into Dr. Bob and spoil all the brownie points I got for volunteering."

I leap to my feet and rush off to where Annabel and I left our bikes. "Nice talking with you, man," Greg shouts after me.

# Chapter Eight

Annabel's bike is gone. I jump on my bike and pedal off, wishing I had a light. The bike is an old ten-speed with narrow tires and dropped handlebars. The track is rough, and it's getting dark fast. My front wheel keeps hitting rocks and slewing the whole bike sideways. I almost wipe out two or three times.

The going gets harder as the track steepens away from the river. I risk a glance at the sky. To the east, I can see stars, but to the west is a solid black mass. The thunderheads have grown to cover half the sky. That's all I need— thunder, lightning and torrential rain. As if to emphasize my thought, there's a flash of lightning deep in the clouds. I don't count, but it's several seconds before I hear the rumble of thunder. The storm is still distant, but it's coming this way.

The bike's front wheel hits a rock, the wheel shoots out to the side, and I make painful contact with the ground. I'm only wearing shorts, so I scrape a huge amount of skin off my right leg. I must have cried out when I fell, because a voice comes at me from the darkness farther up the hillside some-where. "Sam?"

"Annabel," I shout back as I struggle painfully to my feet. "Is that you? Where are you?" They are both dumb questions, but what do you say in a situation like this?

"Yes, it's me," Annabel replies. "I fell off my bike. I've hurt my ankle."

"Okay," I say. "I'm coming. Keep talking."

"I don't feel too good. My ankle hurts, and I bumped my head."

"Recite Pi for me," I say.

I'm relieved to hear the familiar numbers in the darkness—"3.14159265359…"

I head toward them.

A mixture of emotions churns through me as I pick my way toward the voice—relief that I've found Annabel, worry about her ankle, joy that I get to play the knight in shining armor and that Greg is nowhere in sight. I'm not proud of the last emotion, but I can't control the way I feel.

Annabel is a surprisingly long way off the track. "How did you wind up way over here?" I ask as I get closer.

"The track splits back there. I guess I took the wrong one, because it petered out. I tried to turn and fell off my bike."

"You hit your head?"

Annabel raises a hand to her temple. "It's okay. Bit of a lump, and I guess I'll have a nice bruise. It's my ankle that really hurts." Annabel is sitting on a mound of earth, her right leg stretched out in front of her. "It's not too bad if I don't move it," she adds.

"Where's your bike?" I'm thinking she can sit on the bike while I push it back down to the river.

"Over behind me, but it's in rough shape."

I move to where Annabel points. She's right—the bike's front wheel looks as if it's permanently going around a corner. "You really did a number on it,"

I say, coming back to Annabel. "We'll get you down to my bike and then to the river. Let's have a look at your ankle."

It's hard to see in the darkness, but it's obvious that Annabel's ankle is seriously swollen. I run my hand gently over it and hear a sharp intake of breath. "I think it might be broken," she says softly.

"It might just be a bad sprain," I say as positively as possible. "We need to get you where someone can look at it. I'll carry you to the bike."

The flash of lightning and the peal of thunder are much closer together than before. I don't want to get caught out here in the storm. I freeze when I see headlights coming up the rough track.

"Who's that?" I wonder out loud. Help may be on the way, but I have an uneasy feeling.

"Probably kids coming up to party," Annabel says, "but who cares? Go and flag them down."

Heading into a badlands coulee at night in a thunderstorm? That makes them really dumb, even for partying kids. That's what I think. What I say is, "Okay. Wait here. I'll get them to help carry you down." I set off to where I think I'll meet up with the headlights.

The first raindrop hits me square in the middle of the forehead. It feels about the size of a quarter. With terrifying suddenness, the heavens open. It's like standing under a waterfall. I'm soaked through in seconds. The lightning is almost continuous and the thunder feels as if it's coming from the ground below me. Then my feet slide out from under me, and I'm sitting on the slope.

I should run, crawl, slide, do whatever it takes to get to the vehicle that can take Annabel to help, but I don't. I sit on the slope, staring at the track. As I fell, the lightning lit everything up like the noonday sun—the Red Deer River valley to my left, the opening to the coulee to my right and, straight ahead, Darren's truck with the crushed remains of my bike beneath its back wheels.

What I see are isolated scenes lit by the lightning flashes, and they are all out of focus through the curtain of torrential rain. Two people get out of the truck, Darren and the squat figure of Beetlebrow. I can't hear what they're saying, but they move around and look at what's left of my bike. Darren hauls it out and tosses it to one side. Both of them are waving their arms, pointing up the track and at the sky. It looks as if they're arguing about whether to go on.

Then a second vehicle arrives on the scene, the black Hummer. This time they don't go and talk to the driver through the window—the driver gets out and walks toward them. He gestures angrily.

I get a good, lightning-illuminated look at the Hummer driver. He's a short, plump, well-dressed guy wearing thick round glasses. I can't believe what I'm seeing. A black dog sticks its muzzle out the Hummer's partly open window. The dog can only be Percy, and the guy is Humphrey Battleford.

Darren and Beetlebrow climb back into the truck and, tires spinning, head into the coulee, followed by the Hummer. They've disappeared before I think, I should have kept going. I should have attracted their attention. They could have given Annabel a ride. But would they have?

My guess is, the three of them are only up here for one reason—to steal the fossil.

## Chapter Nine

Sliding and slipping, I fight my way back to Annabel. "What happened?" she asked. "I saw the lights stop and then move off again, and there was another vehicle. Have they gone to get help?"

"It was Darren and Beetlebrow in the truck," I say. I have to shout to make myself heard over the noise of the storm.

"That's weird," Annabel says, "but you didn't answer my question. Have they gone for help?"

"No," I say. "The other vehicle was the black Hummer we saw in town."

"That would have been great for getting around in this weather," Annabel says.

"No, it wouldn't," I say. "The Hummer was driven by Humphrey Battleford."

Annabel is silent for a long time. "Are you sure?" she asks finally.

"I got a good look at him in the lightning, and Percy was with him."

"They're after the fossil," Annabel says excitedly. "We have to stop them."

"How?" I'm amazed that Annabel has gone from needing to be rescued to being determined and in charge.

"The rain has eased off."

I look up. She's right. It's not the torrent it was a few minutes ago, and there are gaps between the lightning flashes and the thunder. Not that this makes an immediate difference. I'm still soaked through and shivering, and the ground is still as slippery as ice. "Leave me here and go tell someone what's happening."

I look at Annabel. She's shivering as well. "No. We'll both go."

"Don't be silly. You can't carry me all that way, and the bumping wouldn't do my ankle any good."

"I know," I say, "but you're soaked through, cold and probably in shock. Leaving you here while I walk all the way back isn't an option."

"Then what?"

"I'm going to steal Battleford's Hummer."

"You're crazy."

I probably am, but I explain my plan anyway. "I can carry you down as far as the track. You wait there while I go into the coulee. I'll get the Hummer and come back and pick you up."

"You can't drive."

"I've watched Dad lots of times. How tough can it be? It's not like I'll be driving in heavy traffic." I try to sound confident, but inside, I'm terrified. What if the Hummer's locked? What if it's a stick shift? What if they catch me? I go on before Annabel has a chance to object again. "It'll work, but we have to get you down to the track. You ready?"

"I guess so." Annabel doesn't look sure, but then neither am I.

I help Annabel stand on her good leg. As carefully as I can, I take her piggyback, trying to keep her injured leg as still as possible. I keep to the flattest ground, walking in an awkward shuffle and testing every step before I put weight on it. We make slow progress, and Annabel gasps every time I stumble, but we make it to the track.

I sit Annabel on a mound of dirt. She's breathing heavily and shaking with cold. "Wait here," I order. "I won't be long. See how much of Pi you can recite before I get back."

Annabel nods weakly, and I set off. I'm exhausted, but I force myself to move in a half run. Luckily, the track is much less slippery than the surrounding slopes, and the exercise warms me. I think of Annabel getting colder beside the road. I force myself to go faster.

Darren's truck is turned sideways at the end of the track, headlights shining up the slope at the dig, and the Hummer is parked behind it. I'm hugely relieved to see two things—there are three figures on the slope, and the Hummer's engine is running. I wait for my lungs to stop hurting and my breathing to slow before slipping around the Hummer to the driver's door. I open it and a black mass explodes out, sending me flying to the ground.

Percy is delighted to see me again and frolics wildly, barking and trying to lick me. I'm struggling to fight off the dog and stand up when I hear a shout from the dig. "Percy! How did you get out? What's going on?"

Percy hesitates, torn between responding to his master's voice and showing me how much he loves me. I take the opportunity to lunge for the Hummer, pull myself into the driver's seat and slam the door. It's an automatic. I haul the lever back to *R* for Reverse and press the accelerator. The Hummer shoots backward. It tilts wildly as one of the rear wheels tries to climb the slope of the coulee. In the headlights, I see the three figures waving and sliding down the slope. Percy gambols around them, getting in the way and thinking this new game is wonderful. An annoying beep tells me I don't have my seatbelt on.

I struggle to look over my shoulder as I steer frantically, trying to keep the Hummer on the track. Fortunately, it has a powerful backup light, but I still swing crazily from side to side and feel more than once as if the whole thing is going to tip over. Then I see Annabel, slumped on the ground where I left her. I brake and push the stick into Park. I pray that I can keep control and not kill the person I've come to rescue.

As soon as the Hummer stops, I leap out and haul the back door open. Annabel is barely conscious. Her teeth are chattering and she's mumbling.

"Come on," I say. I put my arm around her and lift her onto her good leg. She cries out in pain, but it makes her more aware of her surroundings. "Hello," she says.

"Hello," I reply. "We have to get into the Hummer."

"Okay," she agrees, "but I have a problem."

"What?" I glance up the coulee, where I can see headlights bouncing toward us.

"I can't remember the next number. I promised Sam I'd keep reciting Pi, but I can't think of the next number. We can't go until I remember it."

"Seven!" I say frantically.

Annabel's brow furrows. "No, I don't think that's it," she says slowly.

"Four! Two! Nine! Five!" I shout numbers at random, panicking as the headlights get closer.

"Five?" Annabel says dreamily. "I think that's it."

"Great," I say, easing her toward the open door. "Now, let's go."

"Five, two, one, three, eight, four…" Annabel is speaking slowly, but she's helping me. "One, four, six, nine, five…" Now I've got her sitting on the edge of the back seat. "One, nine, four, one, five…" As gently as possible, I lift her legs into the Hummer. Even so, she cries out in pain.

"Sorry," I say as I close the door and jump into the driver's seat. The headlights are close now. I find Reverse and we head off on our erratic course down the track. From the back seat I hear, "One, one, six, zero, nine…"

# Chapter Ten

The rain has stopped by the time I reach the bonfire that the barbecuers have started on the riverbank. I find space to turn the Hummer around and manage to skid to a halt outside the circle of firelight. Dr. Bob is sitting on a packing case, and the familiar chords of "Stairway to Heaven" reach me as I fling the door open.

"He didn't wait for us," Annabel says from the backseat.

The music dies and everyone turns to look as I scramble toward them. "Annabel's broken her ankle," I shout. "We need to get her to the hospital." I see Greg in the shadows. "And someone's trying to steal the fossil in the coulee."

For a long moment everyone just stares at me, and then people are running in all directions. Dr. Bob is beside me. "What happened?" he asks. "And where did you get the Hummer?"

"It's Battleford's," I say. "I'll explain on the way to the hospital."

Dr. Bob nods. "We'd better take my truck."

Together we carry Annabel over to the Tyrrell Museum truck. "Take the ATVs and go and see what's happening in the coulee," Dr. Bob orders Greg.

On the way to town, I explain what happened. Dr. Bob listens intently.

At the hospital, two orderlies wheel Annabel in, and a young doctor examines her. He declares that she has mild hypothermia and orders her wet clothing removed. The nurses wrap her in blankets and tell me to give her sips of warm tea. In minutes, she has improved dramatically.

"Just as well you stopped reciting Pi when we got here," I say. "The doctor would have thought you were much worse."

"Reciting Pi is a sign of not being confused," Annabel says with a weak smile.

"Okay." The doctor bustles in. "It's down to X-ray for you. Let's see what damage you did to that ankle. You two might as well go get a cup of coffee," he adds, turning to Dr. Bob and me. "I'll let you know when the X-rays are done."

I squeeze Annabel's hand as she's wheeled out, and Dr. Bob and I go find a vending machine. As soon as we have our warm drinks, Dr. Bob takes out his cell phone and moves off to one side. I slump gratefully into a nearby chair and sigh with relief. Annabel is in good hands. I rescued her. That makes me feel good. I push back all the other confusing thoughts and dwell on that.

Dr. Bob comes back over. "I think we were lucky," he says. "I just talked to Greg. The fossils are still there. I guess you disturbed the thieves before they could load up."

"It's a shame Greg left the site," I say, unable to resist a dig at my rival for Annabel's affection.

"He shouldn't have," Dr. Bob says, "but who could have predicted what happened? Maybe it's just as well he wasn't there when the thieves arrived."

"I suppose so," I say.

"Are you sure it was Battleford you saw?" Dr. Bob asks.

"I got a good look at him in the light-ning, and it was his dog in the Hummer."

Dr. Bob nods. "When did you learn to drive?"

"About two hours ago in the Hummer, coming out of the coulee," I say.

Dr. Bob laughs. "Well, good that you did—although, technically, you stole the Hummer." I hadn't thought of that. Seeing my worried look, Dr. Bob goes on. "I doubt Battleford will press charges. We may not even see him. The police won't have any trouble finding Darren and Beetlebrow, but Battleford is a different matter. If I were him, I'd disappear."

We are interrupted by the doctor. "Nothing's broken," he says as I stand up. "Your friend has a grade two sprain. This means there's ligament damage that may take some time to heal. But with a few days of rest, ice and anti-inflammatories, she should be well on the way to recovery. I've asked the nurse to get a set of crutches and some ice packs. As soon as they're here, you can be on your way."

"Thank you," Dr. Bob and I say at the same time.

Annabel is much better now that she's warm and dry. "You owe me 'Stairway to Heaven,'" she reminds Dr. Bob as he drives us back to the farm. Despite the late hour, Mom and the others fuss over us and demand to hear about our adventures. At last I drop off to sleep, only slightly worried about Humphrey Battleford.

## Chapter Eleven

It's daylight when Mom wakes me from a deep sleep on Sunday morning. "I was going to let you sleep on," she says, "but there's someone here to see you."

"Who?" I ask groggily.

"He didn't give a name. I invited him in for tea, but he said he'd rather wait outside."

As the events of the previous night flood back, I struggle into my clothes, stumble downstairs and go outside. At first, all I can see is a taxi. Then I notice a figure by the fence. He has a black dog on a short leash. It's Humphrey Battleford and Percy.

"What are you doing here?" I ask as he turns toward me. He is smiling, and Percy is straining against his leash.

"I heard you were in the neighborhood, so I thought Percy and I should say hello," he says in his cultured American accent. He's immaculately dressed in a three-piece suit, even though it's already warm.

"I thought you would be long gone by now," I say, "after your failed attempt to steal the fossil." It feels good to point out that Battleford has failed.

"And what gave you the impression that I was trying to steal anything?"

"I saw you," I say triumphantly, "and Percy." I bend to scratch the excited dog's ear. It's not his fault his master's a crook. "Last night in the coulee with Darren and Beetlebrow."

"Beetlebrow?" Battleford looks confused.

"The courier guy with the eyebrows."

Battleford chuckles. "Good name for him," he says.

"Anyway, I'm going to the police this morning to make a full report."

"Commendable of you," Battleford says with a smile. His calmness is unnerving. "But I fear your trip will be wasted. You see, you are mistaken."

"I'm not mistaken," I say. "I saw you."

"You may think you saw me, but in the middle of a storm as violent as the one last night, who can be sure what they see?"

"Percy almost knocked me over."

"Is it not true," Battleford says slowly, "that your friend Darren has a similar breed of dog?"

"He's not my friend, and it *was* Percy and you."

"Hmm." Battleford rubs his chin thoughtfully. "Perhaps I shall accompany you to the police station. You see, my Hummer was stolen last night. I should probably report it. I have to go and pick it up anyway. It's damaged. Only slightly—a few scratches, a dent or two—but these vehicles are terribly expensive to repair. Actually," he says, as if remembering something, "wasn't it you who drove my Hummer to the party by the river?"

"I was bringing an injured person down from the coulee," I say with a sinking feeling in the pit of my stomach.

"Most commendable," Battleford says again, "but failure to ask permission is theft nonetheless."

"So you admit you were in the coulee last night," I say triumphantly.

"Not at all." Battleford is unfazed. "I was dining last night with a colleague in the precious-fossil business, a fact she will confirm. My Hummer was taken from town. Probably kids out joyriding, but that doesn't alter the fact that you were seen driving a stolen vehicle with several thousand dollars' worth of damage to it."

Battleford looks at me carefully. I feel trapped. I've seen what this man's lawyers can do. If he wants me to be liable for the damage to his Hummer, I will be in a lot of trouble. And what do I have? My word that I saw him and his dog under less than ideal conditions at a place where no crime was committed?

"I suggest we forget the whole thing," Battleford says in his silky voice. "After all, no harm was done. You still have your fossil, and I was thinking of selling the Hummer anyway. It uses too much gas, and one must be environmentally conscious these days, don't you think?"

"I suppose so," I say.

"Excellent. Excellent. I shall go and collect my vehicle, and we will say no more about this unfortunate event. Come on, Percy. Time for a walk by the river."

Battleford turns toward the cab.

"What about Darren and Beetlebrow?" I shout after him.

"Ah yes, Darren and Beetlebrow." Battleford half turns and speaks to me over his shoulder. "It seems they were out for a drink on a pleasant evening when they saw someone driving a Hummer in a dangerous manner. Being good citizens, they followed the vehicle on its erratic course but lost contact and headed back to town." He smiles broadly at me. "Goodbye, Sam. I enjoy our little conversations, but I hope this is the last."

I go back into the house to find Annabel sitting at the kitchen table. She has her right leg raised and an ice pack on her ankle. "How's your leg?" I ask.

"A bit better. I slept with it on a pile of pillows, and the swelling's down this morning. Was I a real idiot last night?"

I laugh. "You could reduce your IQ by ninety percent and you'd still be smarter than most people. You were great."

"Thank you for rescuing me," she says. "My knight in shining armor. Where have you been?"

"We had a visitor," I say.

"Who?"

"Two visitors, in fact. Humphrey Battleford and Percy."

"What? Why was he here?" Annabel looks so agitated, I think she's about to jump up on her injured leg and run around the kitchen.

"He came to tell us not to talk about last night."

"We have to," Annabel says. "We have to go to the police. He tried to steal the fossil."

"He did," I agree, "but 'tried to' is the important part of that sentence. We have no evidence that he intended to steal the fossil, and the only crime committed was my stealing his Hummer. He's not the one who'll go to prison if we pursue this. Besides, he says he has an ironclad alibi for last night, dinner with some woman in the valuable-fossil business."

"But…" Annabel's brow furrows in thought. "I guess you're right. Battleford wins again."

"But he didn't get the fossil," I point out, "and Dr. Bob said they were collecting it first thing this morning. It's safe now."

The furrows deepen. "Why do you suppose he went to the effort of telling us to keep quiet if no crime was committed? He had nothing to worry about."

"I don't know. He doesn't like loose ends, I suppose." We fall silent. As I think of loose ends, something else preys on my mind. I have to mention it before it drives me crazy. "How do you feel about Greg?" I ask, dreading the answer.

"Greg?" Annabel drags herself away from her thoughts. "How do I feel about Greg? What do you mean?"

"Do you...like him? Prefer him to me?"

Of all the reactions I'd imagined, laughter was not one. Eventually, Annabel gets herself under control. "Why would I prefer pirate boy to you?"

"He's cool. He's smart. He knows a lot about the same stuff you do—Pi and all that. He's the same height as you."

Annabel shakes her head. "For an intelligent person, you sure are dumb sometimes. Greg is a pompous twit with way too high an opinion of himself. Sure, he knows some stuff that makes him interesting to talk to. This can also be said of Dr. Bob. Are you jealous of him, too?"

"Of course not."

"Come here."

I move around the table and Annabel struggles to stand. I reach out to help and she falls into my arms. We hug, and she kisses me on the cheek. "I find nothing remotely attractive in Greg," she whispers in my ear. "I like my men shorter and a little bit dumb. That way I can feel superior to them."

I laugh and hug Annabel back. A sense of relief washes over me.

Then Annabel pushes me away. "Wait," she says. "What if a crime *was* committed?"

"What do you mean?"

"We have to go to the museum."

"Why?"

"I have to check something."

"How? The bikes are destroyed, and even if they weren't, you can't ride with your ankle."

As if on cue, my mother bustles into the kitchen. "Some of us are going into town in the van," she announces cheerfully. "You guys want to tag along?"

"Yes. No," I say. "Can you drop us off at the museum?"

"Sure," Mom says. "You up for that, Annabel?"

"I'm fine," Annabel says. "I just need my crutches.

Confused but happy, I follow the others as we all pile into the ancient Volkswagen van and chug off toward town.

## Chapter Twelve

"We need to see Dr. Bob." Even on crutches, Annabel is an unstoppable force of nature. I don't think the receptionist even considers not doing as she's asked. Within minutes, Dr. Bob appears through a nearby *Staff Only* door.

"Good morning," he says cheerily. "You both look better than last night. How's the ankle?"

"Fine. Did you collect the fossils this morning?"

Dr. Bob looks taken aback by Annabel's abrupt question. "Yes," he says. "We went up first thing and loaded them. They're in storage in the back."

"Can I see them?"

"Sure, but why?"

"I want to see something."

Dr. Bob shrugs, as much in the dark as I am, and leads the way. Annabel clumps impatiently along behind him.

The three lumps of white plaster are at eye level on the blue shelving. Annabel leans forward and studies the one that contains the skull for a moment. "They've been switched," she announces, stepping back.

Dr. Bob and I stare at her.

"This isn't the fossil. The casts have been switched."

"That's impossible," Dr. Bob says when he finds his voice. "They were where we left them. They're the right size and shape. They even have the correct identifying information on them." He points to the location and date information written in black marker on the top.

"They don't have any Pilish on them." We both stare stupidly at Annabel. "Greg and I made up a Pilish saying and wrote it along the edge of the skull cast. *Now I find a skull anciently in clever rocks.* He said you wouldn't mind," she finishes weakly.

"I don't," Dr. Bob says, peering at the cast. "Where did you write it?"

"Here." Annabel runs her finger along the bottom edge of the cast.

"Are you certain?"

"Absolutely."

Dr. Bob leans forward and taps the cast several times. Then he scratches the surface with his fingernail. "You're right," he says eventually. "The composition is different from the mix we use at the museum." He takes a pocket knife out of one of his many pockets and digs a small hole through the cast. "Not even the right kind of rock," he says. "Looks like this is a boulder from some farmer's field." He folds the knife and steps back. "How did they do this? They are the same size and shape as the real casts. There wasn't enough time to make these fake ones last night."

"Greg helped," Annabel says.

"Greg?" Dr. Bob and I say together.

"Not intentionally," Annabel says, "but remember his daily blog? He posted photos of every stage of the process. With those and the details Darren had from hanging around, plus what Beetlebrow knows of fossil casts, they could make copies. The exchange on the coulee wouldn't have taken long. Then they loaded the real fossils into Darren's truck."

"So the fossils will be in Darren's barn," I say.

"Not necessarily," Annabel says. "Remember Battleford's alibi for last night?"

"Dinner with someone," I say.

"A woman in the valuable-fossil business, you said," says Annabel.

"The woman from Precious Fossils and Gems," I say.

"It seems like a fair bet," Annabel agrees. "Battleford must have seen her at some point after they took the fossil, if only to get his alibi straight, and I bet he'd rather leave something valuable with her than with Darren and Beetlebrow."

"Luela Harmsworth-Lewis," Dr. Bob informs us. "She would know where to send the fossils for preparation. Probably even which courier company to use. I've often had suspicions about her. She has too many high-quality specimens. We need to call the police."

"Yes," Annabel agrees, "but that might not be enough. It'll take time to get a search warrant for Precious Fossils and Gems."

"You think Battleford will take the fossils away as soon as he gets the Hummer back?" I ask.

"Possibly, but he likes to distance himself from the shadier dealings of his associates. I doubt he'd want stolen fossils in the back of his vehicle, especially if he has to cross the border."

"So they'll be in the back room of Luela's shop," I say.

Annabel is not listening. She's clumping toward the open overhead loading door at the back of the storage area.

"I doubt Luela will want stolen property on her premises for long," she says over her shoulder. "She'll want to get rid of them as soon as possible, probably using a courier service."

Annabel stops on the edge of the loading dock and points at the panel van parked to one side. The dark red with gold lettering on the side reads *Paterson Scientific Courier Service—Nothing Too Big or Too Small*.

"Beetlebrow's van!" I exclaim.

"I'll bet you a supersized full-meal deal the fossils are in there," Annabel says.

"Then let's go and see." Dr. Bob jumps down and hauls on the van's back door. It's not locked, and it doesn't take us long to find the three plaster casts, complete with Pilish writing.

"How quickly can the police get here?" I ask.

"I don't think we need the police," Annabel says. We both stare at her. "Battleford has expensive lawyers. We know that," she says to me. "No one went to prison for stealing the *Loch Ard* peacock. No one will go to prison for this. There isn't enough hard evidence." Annabel turns to Dr. Bob. "Remember Sue?"

"Yes," Dr. Bob says thoughtfully. "That case dragged through the courts for years. Different situation, but good lawyers can make simple matters complicated."

"If we don't go to the police," I say, "Battleford gets away with it."

"Not if we switch the casts back," Annabel says with a smile.

"Perfect," Dr. Bob says. "We get the important fossil back, Battleford gets nothing and Beetlebrow ends up looking for another job. We'd better hurry. I'll get some help." He runs off to round up a few summer students.

It only takes minutes for a sheepish Greg and a couple of others to make the exchange and close up the van. Moments later, Beetlebrow shows up, looks around sullenly and drives off.

"I'd love to be a fly on the wall when the lab cuts off the plaster to find only boulders inside," Dr. Bob says as we watch. "Come on, I'll buy you two lunch."

# Chapter Thirteen

*"And she's buying a stairway to Heaven."*
The last chords of "Stairway to Heaven"
drift off into the warm prairie evening.

"It's not Led Zeppelin," Annabel
says, "but a very decent cover."
Tomorrow we drive into Calgary for the
long flight back to Australia. Dr. Bob
has organized this farewell barbecue on
the banks of the Red Deer River.

"Dr. Bob is certainly a man of many talents," I agree. "Have you enjoyed the holiday?" After the first frantic days, our two weeks in Alberta have been calm. With a few day's rest, Annabel's ankle has improved dramatically. Not enough to hike in the Rocky Mountains, but Dr. Bob took us to the incredible Dinosaur Provincial Park at Brooks. Mom took us to renew our psychic energy at Head-Smashed-In Buffalo Jump. With trips to see the sights of Calgary, we have had a full time.

"It's been great," Annabel says. "I love your Mom, and I learned a lot at all the places we've been. There's only one regret."

"What's that?" I ask, concerned at the sad expression she's suddenly wearing.

"Well," she says, close to tears. "I really would have liked to spend more time with Greg."

I dig her playfully in the ribs and we both laugh. Greg has kept a low profile since he discovered that his blog had helped the attempted theft. "One thing bothers me," I say. "Back in the Museum store room, if Battleford had written the Pilish on the cast, what would you have done?"

"Smashed it open," Annabel says matter-of-factly.

"You were that certain?"

"Yeah," she says. "Never underestimate Battleford."

Dr. Bob strolls over and sits beside us.

"Awesome," Annabel says.

"Thank you," Dr. Bob says with a smile. "Compliment indeed from someone your age. I do think I shall move away from classic rock and check out some of the indie rock bands around"

"Any news on the police investigation?" I ask.

"They've questioned Beetlebrow, and he's leading them to a ring that illegally sells valuable fossils. I think Luela will be in serious trouble."

"Nothing that leads back to Battleford?" Annabel asks.

"Dr. Bob shakes his head. "He's Teflon-coated, nothing sticks to him. That reminds me, this arrived for you at the museum this afternoon."

Dr. Bob produces a gift-wrapped box from his bag and hands it over. It feels heavy for its size, but there's nothing written on it. Annabel unwraps it. Nestled in tissue paper is a beautiful coiled fossil shell, its polished surface gleaming in the firelight.

"That's a lovely ammonite," Dr. Bob says. "Jurassic in age, I would guess. Who's it from?"

Annabel lifts a gold-edged embossed card from the box. *"For my two young friends. Thank you for the entertainment and the scratches behind the ear. All the best, Percy.*"

"It's from Battleford," I say. "He's taunting us."

"I think he enjoys almost getting caught," Annabel comments, turning the fossil over in her hands. "Life must get boring when you're rich enough to have anything you want. I wonder if we've seen the last of him."

# Author's Note

The Royal Tyrrell Museum in Drumheller, Alberta, has one of the best collections of fossils in the world, and it *is* possible to look into a *T. rex*'s jaws. It is also possible to climb inside the world's biggest *T. rex* and look down on the rest of the town. The badlands also exist, and at places like Dinosaur Provincial Park near Brooks, Alberta, it is sometimes difficult to walk around without stepping on a dinosaur bone washed down from the surrounding slopes.

I in no way mean to suggest that the fossils you can find in any rock shop are stolen. The vast majority are collected perfectly legally from sites that have been well researched by scientists and prepared by people who love making these incredible remnants of the past visible and available for people to see and own. Unfortunately, however, there is also a thriving underground business in rare and exotic fossils, and some wonderful specimens only exist in the basements and houses of people like Humphrey Battleford.

The characters in *Bones* are fictional, as are some of the locations, such as the back rooms of the Tyrrell Museum and the coulee on Sam's mom's farm. But who knows? Maybe one day a storm will wash out the strange bones of a smart dinosaur from the walls of a coulee somewhere.

John Wilson is the author of numerous stories for young people, including *Stolen,* the first Sam and Annabel adventure in the Orca Currents series. He travels the country extensively, telling stories from his books and getting young readers (particularly but not exclusively boys) energized and wanting to read and find out more about the past. For more information, visit www.johnwilsonauthor.com.

# orca currents

For more information on all the books
in the Orca Currents series, please visit
**www.orcabook.com.**